RED CATS

English versions

by **ANSELM HOLLO**

City Lights Books

These poems were published originally in Russian in

LITERATURNAYA GAZETA
LITERATURNAYA MOSKVA
OKTYABR
NOVY MIR
YUNOST
DEN POESII
and others

The Pocket Poets Series is published by
City Lights Books
261 Columbus Avenue, San Francisco 11, California, USA
Overseas distributors: The Scorpion Press,
Manor House, Pakefield Street, Lowestoft, Suffolk, England.

CONTENTS

Introduction

In the middle 50's a number of Soviet writers started what became known as "The Thaw": a movement towards freedom of personal literary and critical expression that has been going on ever since, in spite of several setbacks and sometimes heavily-worded official censure. YEVGENI YEVTUSHENKO and ANDREI VOZNESENSKY, the two younger poets in this selection, came onto the literary scene during this period. SEMYON KIRSANOV has long represented the most genuinely progressive wing of Soviet Russian poetry, never losing touch with the international revolution in modern literature (the way many of his countrymen unfortunately have lost it, in the thickets of Social Realism or Romanticism).

YEVGENI YEVTUSHENKO, now 28 years old, is the first Soviet poet since Mayakovsky who has the makings of a great public figure. In recent years he has traveled much abroad, as a mouthpiece for his own (and, we hope, his generation's) brand of Individualistic Communism. . . . Despite its comparatively narrow line-of-attack, his long poem "Babi

Yar" expresses something of the poetic kinship Yevtushenko says he feels with Allen Ginsberg, the American poet he "loves best": it is a moving indictment of racism in Russia and everywhere, and, by implication, of all forms of oppression and intolerance.

ANDREI VOZNESENSKY is in his middle twenties, "a poet of the Generation of Cosmonauts", as the good Soviet critic Korneli Selinski says in a recent survey of the contemporary Russian poetry scene. "He never looks at anything from in front: his principle seems to be to 'walk round and have a good look', but he moves in parabola, not happy circumferences." Harsher words came from Vsyelovod Kotchetov, author of novels such as "The Secretary of the District Committee": he recently called Voznesensky and his contemporary Yevtushenko "pale-beaked chickens of poetry who are trying hard to strut and swagger like little fighting-cocks . . ."

Among their books:

Semyon Kirsanov: "Selected Poems 1923-1957"
                     "Tracks in the Sand" 1960
Andrei Voznesensky: "Mosaic", Poems 1960

Yevgeni Yevtushenko: "Explorers of the Future"
1960

"Morning Poems" in
"Poems of Various Years"
1959

"The Apple" 1960

To Lawrence Ferlinghetti who had the idea: to Maud Arvidson, Edwin Morgan, Natalie Tarassow and Iris Walden who helped me realize it: to Allen Ginsberg for the title: to Semyon Kirsanov, Yevgeni Yevtushenko and Andrei Voznesensky for their good poems: to Vladimir Mayakovsky who was a lover: to Josephine, in whom I love the world: one word: Thankyou!

—*Anselm Hollo*

14.4.1962

Yevtushenko :

AGAINST BORDERS

All these borders—
they
bug me! Nothing
do I know
of Buenos Aires, or
New York
—and I should
know! I should be able to go
to London
and walk around,
and talk to the people,
even if I can't talk so good,
just walking
around. Like a little kid
I want to ride a bus
through Paris
some morning,
and I want an art
that is something
else, is an exciting sound—
like myself!

—1958

Yevtushenko:

I SAW HIM

As we were sitting in that waiting-room
at Copenhagen Airport
like having some coffee in modern surroundings
real comfortable, elegant, tired surroundings
all of a sudden
there was this man, this old guy
in a rough green duffel-type jacket
with a face burnt away by salt and wind—
it was not as if he'd come in
he just appeared,
rolled through the tourist crowd
as if he'd just come off the boat,
a helmsman, his beard like meerschaum
white, a fringe all around that face.
Parting the people in a big wave
determined and grouchy he moved
through the old time that leads to the new
through all that modernity that's really decrepit—
had a vodka, straight
at the bar: the skin on his hands looked parched
and cracked, his shoes
were the kind that make a hell of a noise

his pants had never been to the cleaners, and yet
he looked great.
                    He looked a damn sight greater
than all those elegant hippies around him.
The floor seemed to give
like the planks on a ship—
                              he really walked
the earth . . .
                    And one of the guys I was with
gave me a nudge and said, "Look at that
—like some Hemingway . . ."
And he walked off,
the whole hulk of a man, and that hulk
was everywhere, in his tiniest gesture
with that fisherman's gait
the granite fisherman
—like walking off through a hail of bullets
dodging the low-slung lamps like a man bent double
in trenches, pushing aside tables and people
that were in his way,
yes, he really looked like "a Hemingway".
And later I heard
whom I'd seen,
                    I had seen
                              Hemingway.

                                        —1961

Yevtushenko :

URIAH HEEP
— a London Poem —

It's sad : but Mr Heep
ain't dead. Here he is, feebly grinning, rabbity eyes
an albino checking our passports
here he is, digging into our luggage
our shirts—the tins of caviar—
disappearing into the suitcase with huge wet ears
that seem to be growing longer all the time . ..
He's looking
for something, some kind of bonus.
Perhaps
the H-Bomb? ?
He can't find it. Says, "Here you are" shrugging
drops out of our sight—
Forgive me, England
yes forgive me for starting my poem like this !
I met such great people there
yes really good people, I have to call them my own !
But still, but still
that creep Uriah Heep is still with us—
he must have holed up somewhere,

he's still around
cheering the neo-fascists, heap lot of good
that'll do him
writing weird articles in the Daily Mail
putting down everybody
who still isn't for sale.
Coming on strong about "morals," all that.
Putting down Mr Pickwick,
really running poor Mr Pickwick into the ground.
Looking at me
as if he was going to sell me the Keys
of the Kingdom—sexless, creepy
he terrifies me!
I've heard people say, who come on like thinkers
that genius and creepiness
are immortal . . .
I dunno. Anyway, Heep, I think one day
we'll stand by your grave,
England and I,
much closer together under this sky!

London 1961

Semyon Kirsanov :

MAYAKOVSKY HAS GONE

"The Poem—
—all poetry—
a journey to The Unknown"
—*Mayakovsky*

The Polytechnic Museum
News stalls
A tram-car.
A poster:
"MAYAKOVSKY"

The evening is over.
A hundred steps
down,
he is coming
down.
Surrounded by fans.

A glowing butt
in the corner of his mouth.
He is staring
in front of himself
with burning
eyes.

Notes in his hand.
A blanket over his arm.

Screeching
  is time
torn off
  the two engines . . .

In his pocket
  the crimson passport
and ticket,
  already punched
for the journey
  into the future.
MAYAKOVSKY
  is raising his eyes
    to the sky,
      it is dawn—
        his chestnut
          eyes,
          coming out of a hundred years' wake . . .

At last—he gets up.
  He gets up, he gets going,
he is on his way
  around the world,

and for ever.
He gets on the plane,
    followed
        by sacks of airmail,
now
    his feet
        do not touch
            our globe
                any more.

But still
    from the
hermetic
    door:
—Remember—
    keep in touch—
    one way
    or the other—

And he was gone.
    Was it to the new
or to the old world?
    no matter

    no letters came,

ten,
     twelve,
          thirteen,
               forty years

—1950

Semyon Kirsanov:

THE POEM

A man.
　　Inside,
he is weeping.
　　A crumpled
envelope
　　in his hand.

A hundred steps
　　up, he moves
on the escalator.
　　Up to the columns
and the bright hall
　　—all kinds of men
are floating
　　with lowered
heads
　　up from the subway—

I see he is losing
　　the ground
that was under
　　his feet.

He is floating past
   marble wreaths
on the walls
   of this splendid
white vault . . .

   But he doesn't want
to see this
   marvelous hall
in motion.
   His eyes
—no one must notice!—
   are fighting
against the daggers
   of tears . . .
Should I
   go to him,
perhaps say—
   "Anything wrong?"

   No good.
No slow-moving talk
   is going to
help him.
   But perhaps—

poetry
would?
A poem,
rushing
hot to the rescue—
to take away
grief,
the burden
of worry,
even the
greatest
pain—

to help him
get his foot back
on the threshold
to make him
rise
back to life,

on the small stairs
of its lines!

Yevtushenko:

FROM THE PORTRAIT
OF A "NIHILIST"

He wore his pants
    tapered,
hip. He dug Hemingway

too. But his father
    said glumly
"Son, your taste

    is *un-Russian . . .*"
Thus he saddened
    his family

    hard-working
boosters of output—
    all the time

arguing with them
    about these weird
predilections.

—1960

Yevtushenko :

THE HOODS

So this is the Great Twentieth,
Century of the Sputnik.
What a scarey and scared century
it is!
A fine century
And a century of quicklime and pits . . .
A century with many
fine ideas.
A century that eats those ideas again.
A century to be hated
by those who are young in it—
yes, they hate it, all right.
Their looks could murder it all right.
They hate their governments,
they hate their politics,
they don't like the Church too much—
they don't have much use for philosophers,
and they don't have much use for women either,
except for sleeping with them
once in a while.
They don't much like the world,
to tell the truth.

They don't much like its banks and cashiers,
they don't like themselves,
for not liking anything much,
they know,
they know all about it, that misery.
The Great Twentieth is just their bad, old,
stepfather.
They hate him all right!
And their hatred is black and strong,
moving fast, beating along
the dark banks of the Hudson,
the Tiber, the Seine,
or the Thames,
they are moving, they are there, they're the same,
black shiny dogs from the same kennel.
They're tough, they're hip, they're cool
and they're very strange,
this is the first century they've ever been here.
And I can see through their eyes,
I can see what they
don't want to have any part of,
there's nothing wrong with that vision.
But what do they want?
What are they waiting for?
Or could it be—
they just want to go on sneering and putting

it all down,
to be put down themselves,
and that's about it?
Then I want to say this to them: talking
plain talk: no shit, here I am,
in this City of Moscow
and I too have my hates
and many things to be scared of,
yet I know they're all part of what I Love!
and what has loved me!
though it has some evil faces,
and I make a noise against those,
a big noise, sometimes,
trying to shout them down!
But not shouting
a dull nothing sneer.
I know there is truth, somewhere,
there is, in this century, too,
there is truth in what Lenin said
there is truth in the things you can work with,
like hammers and plows.
And when I come fighting, here,
I know I'm fighting for friends,
I'm fighting for them, even
when I'm fighting against them.
But you,

what happened
to you?
Is it some truth like this
you are waiting for, scowling, in pain,
standing there? "Mass psychosis"—sure thing,
that's what the brainshrinkers say,
shrugging. And you go on shuffling
across two continents,
on the road in Europe
on the American road . . .
The Great Twentieth: the Sputnik—
Century,
you're not dead yet!
Why don't you live things up
why don't you shake them up
and out of that endless, sinister groove?
Don't hand them any "security" crap, Century,
give them something to grab hold of—
something like a belief
in the right things, the good things you have!
They're not your enemies, Century.
These kids, your kids can't be enemies.
You've got to do something for them,
do you hear me,

you've got to give,
you've got to give them a new road!
I'm talking to you, Century.

Yevtushenko :

POEM FOR A YOUNG GIRL

All the kids
making passes
at you,
after the lecture—so many
great things
to do, like
dates and
going to a play and
having flowers sent
to you. But
what you want
most of all, best
of all, is not
so easily found

—there
you go, up
the stairs
in quick spurts.
Eighteen.
The Komsomol
Youth Card

in your hand-
bag, with Lenin's
Profile, Embossed.
I know:
when midnight
is ticking
over and into
morning
in your
silent house,
you hope for another
companionship, from great
and demanding
ideas; stand there
unwinding your tresses
... your thoughts
of revolution, a love
that is all and enough.
In your silent
house, as time
marches by
on its pendulum legs, you
talk to your soul.

You're still very small

you are tiny
beside me, who am very
big! I am
huge, beside you, you
and I, you
the younger, I
the "elder"—and
worried
in my older head,
about yours,
under that pretty
blond hair; your head
that is driving you
driving you into a
torment
for a view
from the heights;
and
I have started to
believe again, in
many things,
just to help you
believe them, too.

—1956

Yevtushenko :

TWO MORNING POEMS

I

How terrible : closing your eyes
to the life around you
you pronounce solemn, suspicious judgment
on Youth!
Yes, its actions are vague
and uncertain.
No evil secret
in that old truth—
But a blind judge is useless
and it is bad enough
to see a friend
in one who hates you
—worse still : to see
an enemy in one who is your friend.

II

They accuse me
of many things.
There are many around
who don't love me at all.
They want to strike me
with lightning and thunder!
I can hear their sinister laughter
flapping its wings overhead.
I can feel their venomous stares
snaking across my shoulders.
   But I tell you,
I get a big charge out of this—
their raging just goes to show
that they
can't make it!

—1958

Yevtushenko:

FROM A TALK

They tell me: "Man
you are *brave*!"
And I'm not—bravery never was my vice.
I just didn't feel low enough
to be quite as cowardly as some I saw around.
But I never tried to push the world out of orbit.
I just wrote.
So what?
I never informed, though.
And I laughed at what was too much—poked fun
                                   at the Bogus—
      tried to say what I thought—loud enough to be
                                      heard.
But a time will come to remember
and burn with shame:
When we shall have done with dishonesty and
                                    plain lies
with those strange times when a man who was
                                 simply honest
was called "brave"!

Semyon Kirsanov :

THE NEW HEART

I'm busy!
I am building
  a model, of an entirely
    new
      heart!

A heart
  for the future : to feel
    and love with. A heart
      to understand men with :

And also, to tell me, whom
  I should freely
    shake by the hand—
and to whom
  I should never
    extend it.

—1956

Andrei Voznesensky :

GOYA

I am Goya: my eyes are destroyed
by enemy beaks.
Shell-holes stare from the naked field.

I am misery,

the Voice of War
the voice of charred cities' timber
on the snow of the Year
Forty-one.

I am the old woman's throat
who was hung, whose body sang like a bell
over the naked townsquare . . .

I am Goya.
Grapes of Wrath! Dust
I am, raised by the barrage in the West.
Dust of the intruder . . .

And bright stars

were hammered in the memorial sky

like nails.

Yes, I
am Goya.

Andrei Voznesensky :

— SPARKS —

A spark of
      research
A spark of
      risk
A spark of Godlike
        insolence

Can set fire
      to a heart
Can burn it out
Can destroy
      the Earth
        for the Devil

Andrei Voznesensky :

FROM THE WINDOW OF A PLANE

In the world of friends
    where travel is slower
what are you doing,
    in the world
of rain?
    With whom are you sharing
a tangerine?
    Or tearing
up notes for a test
    to be taken again?

    You, pretty witch
& Merciless Lady
    —still tossing that mane?
Raising your eyebrows ...
    Or running,
like hammers
    inside a piano
down past the railings,
    the grove of pillars ...
O my beautiful lady

are you still tossing
    that charm around?
Or is it chilled feet
    crossing & crossing
a cold dark room
    —passing & passing
the telephone
    in a zone of gloom
the receiver black,
    heavy, a dumbbell . . .

    Yes I have heard
you are married,
    and I am about
to forget you.
    Why is it then
that I see you again
    cold in that world below,
rushing by
    in the soft sweet rain
that is freezing
    the wing, you come
to mind's eye?

                —1960

Andrei Voznesensky:

THE BIG FIRE AT THE ARCHITECTURAL COLLEGE

There's a fire
in the Architectural!
Those halls!
Those drawings all
on fire! like letters of amnesty
on fire! on fire!

Like a red-ass gorilla
up there on the sleepy façade—
the window,
uncoiling, roaring
to fight—to open
on fire!

We've been studying
for our finals, yes
it's time to defend our thesis!
My pronouncements already crackling
in the sealed
safe—

Like a huge bottle
of kerosene—

five summers, five winters
swoosh up in flames
O my sweet Karen,
O we're on fire!

The little notes
for cheating at tests, the parties
all gone, going-gone, up up
in these flames—
there you stand, pink
                    in the blueberry patch—
goodbye, goodbye!

Farewell Architecture!
Farewell in flames
you cowsheds with little Cupids
you Savings Banks in baroque!
O youth O Phoenix

O stupid, on fire
is your final certificate!
O youth you're waggling your ass
in a red skirt, O youth
you're wagging your tongue—

Farewell, time of boundary
measurements! This is life

—moving on from one burning lot
to another—we're all
on fire, you live—

                        you're on fire!

What winches, what mainstays
will be born in this fire—
to run across
the sheets of Whatman's Paper
like the first tracks
of ski?

But tomorrow, twittering
like an evil bird
and angrier than a hornet
the pair of compasses will be found
in a handful of ashes, and
sting . . .

Everything's burnt down now,
good.
        Everybody
draw a real deep breath.
Everything over?
                    Everything's started!
Now, let's go see
that movie.   —1960

Andrei Voznesensky :

"A NEW YEAR'S LETTER"

A.L.

These guests! heavy
    like hot-water bottles—
all in a row
    on their napkins
their hands lie, red
    like lobsters
on a plate . . .
    And you! lost
among these enormous
    bowls, cooling
your cheek
    on a wine-glass—
off comes
    your shawl,
you're burning! "It's so
    hot in here—"
But back at my place
    the window's
wide open, on the tall
    city, as onto
a garden—and the snow

smelling like
apples, yellow
   Antonowka apples
its flakes
   suspended
in air,
   they don't move
they don't fall
   they're waiting,
weightless, static,
   observant
like small icon
   lamps, or tobacco
plants in summer:
   but they'll swing
in small arcs
   when touched
by a little foot
   in a smart Polish boot . . .
and the snow
and the smell of apples.

—1961

Semyon Kirsanov :

LOVERS' MEETING

Two hours
  to go ...
I walked
  around
in the snow;
  nothing there,
    a few tall pines
      and more snow
        coming down
          all the time.

Then, two hours
  until you came ...
It seemed
  too long, surely
the Volga
  was freezing—

It was like another
  Ice Age,
the very air hard
  the earth encrusted
in a painful shroud.

When I
  saw you,
I saw it was April,
  the air
    breaking out into green—
forget-me-nots on the ground,

the whole world
  petalling out
    around you
who had come to return light
  to all colors.
    It had been four hours :
      There was no such thing
      as ice!

Semyon Kirsanov :

YOUR EYES

You have such eyes . . .
    As if each had two pupils—
the latest make?
    As when at night the cars
of the latest make
    are flying along the highways,
big roaring birds—

    You have eyes
for more than one face,
    enough for two :
and the ocean is shimmering
    with your eyes multiplied
by two and more than two

Do you see what I want to say?
    Your eyes—
maps of two globes :
    when you close them
the tropics are drowned in night
    but when I ask you to open them
I can see the two poles

sky-blue, in their moment
of flowering.

  And I was created
to see you, suddenly here
  on this beach:
and the ocean was given
  to shimmer in front of you
with a million mirrors,
  to soften the ground
for your feet with the grass
  that grows in the sea,
in the watery winds—

  And the airplane was built
to carry me through the air
  —four engines
four trumpets of Jericho
  to bring me here
to land on the earth
  where you
had just been created.

  And before you, perhaps
    no one.

And the world
was created
to create you !
for me to see.

—1960

Semyon Kirsanov :

THE DISTANCES

What are you
Distances
but empty ravines
blind fathomless gorges
deep moats
by steep castle walls ?

But love
needs highways
roads streets
and gates
for us to pass through
on our way
to our meeting :
And if no highways
no roads,

then perhaps forests
   or fields
or hilltops—
   so that we can stumble
along and
   find each other,
make love . . .

   But there are road-blocks,
barriers
   behind them: Guards—

Stop! Answer me:
   where are the bridges
leading to you
   across empty gorges
rivers, desolate moats?

   What? Is not love
enough?
   to raze
all the barriers
   strangling
our roads?

—1960

Semyon Kirsanov :

A LOVE POEM

But white my love
I am white : the chalk that was sea
with fishes and birds
turned white,
white. I am the Cambrian Age
covered with mussel-trails,
my palm the imprint
of some ancient leaf.
But you my love you
are the very beginning
the dance of the dragonfly
the song of the flying fish.
You are the first cloud of thunder
you are life opening its eyes
for the first time in time,
the rainbow, the light's
first mistress, the eyes
that just opened, the flight
of the first bees.
Yet, chalk . . .
my love, and I
am chalk : images in my mind

of bygone birds,
dragonflies,
fishes.
And as you are playing
with pebbles that lie
on my hard white skin
you will read:
                "I loved you."
                              —1960

Semyon Kirsanov :

BUT I WILL BE GONE

But I will be gone
       beyond the horizon
and you will be gone
       beyond the horizon

       But you will be gone
beyond the horizon
       like the day—

But I will be gone
   beyond the horizon
       like the shadow
   is gone
       when the day is moving
   away, across
                   the dunes

Yevtushenko :

SHE

Feel like lying down, yes
lying down to laze in the sun—
it's damp; what the hell, got my spade to lean on. . . .
And a stalk, a nice sour stalk to chew on. . . .
Who wants to go on all day,
breaking his spade and his back
on this rocky ground?
Feel like lying down,
getting some sleep.
But that's what they call wishful thinking.
Just listen to this:
"Hey—what's-a-matter—
can't you stand up any more? Just look at him,
look at that poor, sick, little dovey-boy!!"
Yeah. That's her. Her
in her boots
and her shirt . . . like two round clouds
in that skyblue shirt . . . there
she goes—
"Going to find me a man, yes,
and ooohh, what I'm going to do!
the things I'm going to do

to that poor
man!"—waving her spade around
jingling her ear-rings,
coming on mean and funny, really breaking them up,
"What a mama, hey, what a mean little mama,
just listen to that hot talk!"
Yeah: we know: I know, and the stars know
and the currant bushes—
At night, when the currant leaves are smelling so
   good and strong
we're off to the woods, and you should see her
swimming there in the tall grass,
moving there, like she was
stoned, all smiles and softness;
brown arms falling down and across my back, and
her mouth talking different things
now, beautiful words, beautiful, mixed-up words. . . .
                                        —1957

Yevtushenko :

THE COMING OF SUMMER

At dawn I get up, go out on the porch
    —the wind comes wheeling, to smack me
in the face—
    and by the trees, by the pond, the ground
is covered with flowers. The wind has a breath
    of moist happiness, and then
I feel the earth breathing too,
    on my skin. In the transparent cluster
of trees the birds are swarming and chattering,
    mists are crawling away into nothingness
across the new grass. And there
    seeping through eyelids of sleepy shutters
the glow of dawn
                        entering the cool houses.

I go out on the fields, boots moving
    with ease—all morning I heard
the engines' growl, I go out in the woods
    hear the axe singing duets with its own echo.
Rafts on the pale blue river.
    Sunrays thrown upward in fountains.
Gardens I see full of splendor—

today their bloom
is withering, falling : tomorrow
    will be the first Day of Fruit!
They will hang there,
    like prizes!
fat with warm juices—

It is only spring,
    only a beginning . . .
The creeks make xylophone music
    on the firm tongues of stone in their beds.
The world is a ship, trembling
by the quay—ready, all is ready
for the high seas . . .

    Crows are shrieking above the black fields, rain
is whipping the soil, and the heart
    is beaten on, by the blood
of unwritten songs.
    Day after day my country moves closer to me.
I will give it my life, all I have,
    my death, all I ever will have.
The distances—coming closer—
    the song that arose and flew
across the world—

56

It is only spring
only spring
Spring—a beginning.

Yevtushenko :

RUSSIAN NATURE

How slow
  you are
Russian nature!
  Your waters move
    slow as honey, turning
    slow mills
        mills, very slow . . .
How pitiful,
  Russian nature
before you
  prophet
I am, in eternal
  hurry —
Without rushing about
without pushing it
  you will win
    with your masterful slowness.

I see a grave
    filtering the light,
an owl perched on a branch
    all day: her eyes will make
my fate fade away
    where traffic lights spread
their phosphorescent glow
    like toy city lights
lilies of the valley grow ...
When my time comes
    don't be sad,
go without grieving!
    I will not die.
You, Russian nature
slow Russian nature
    take me
            to yourself!

Yevtushenko :

BABI YAR

Babi Yar
has no mausoleum.
Catacomb
is this ravine.
I stand here, afraid
surrounded by death.
I stand here, old
as a Jew,
as the Jew
crucified!
see my hands,
crucified! Dreyfus
howled at
spewed upon
by a mob
of judges,
imprisoned, walled in
insulted, beaten.
   Women
      in sweet frilly dresses
      poking their parasols
      in my face.

      Shrieking
      with hate.
I stand here
I am the kid
in Byolostok
watching the puddle
of blood on the floor
the tough guys have spilled,
their vodka
cursing us
in their veins
making them deaf
to everything but
that roar :
      BEAT THE KIKES !
      KEEP RUSSIA CLEAN !
      They take
      the boot
      to my mother.
O you Russians
you never held
with such things as frontiers
and creeds
to divide one man
from another.
But those among you

who soiled their hands crimson
have often shouted
your name—
the Russian people: yes
"The Russian People's League"
—a bunch
of haters!
I stand here
I am Ann Frank
a green twig
of a girl, as easy
to tear
off the flowering branch,
of love, of her love
that was natural
and a fullness.
I stand here
   I look at you
   at myself
   it is hard to see
   anything, other
   trees, no trees, no
   leaves, no sky
   —but this rushing
   sound in our ears—

—the boots—
already?
No, it is April.
Coming to find us out,
mouth against mouth
in a small dark room . . .
—but who
is that—
rapping against
the door—
No, it is the river.
Breaking
to flow
with Spring. . . .
It is very quiet now
as I stand here.
Inside me
someone
is howling,
silently,
over the whispering grass
under the tall trees.
The trees
are judges
in black.

I take off my cap
to see
my hair turning gray,
and the howl
inside me
pushes out
through my pores! for
the millions,
who lie here,
faceless.
I stand here
   I lie here
   an old man
   snuffed out
   by the machine-gun's
   deadly spout
   a young man
   who had
   a wife
   a young wife
   who had a
   son
   snuffed out
   by the spurting lead
They have entered

my skin, these people
my veins
and my bones,
they have made my body
their catacomb.
They were Jews.
And this place cannot hear
The International's
fierce booming voice
until the last hater
of these people
lies covered
with earth,
this place
will be deaf
to that song.
I stand here
   I was not born
   a Jew
   but those
   who hated
   and hate
   the blood
   that was shed here
   —they hate

me, as I
have hated them
all my life,
and that
is what makes me
a Russian.

—1961